Charles B. Lines

Memorial of Edward C. D. Lines

Charles B. Lines

Memorial of Edward C. D. Lines

ISBN/EAN: 9783337082093

Printed in Europe, USA, Canada, Australia, Japan

Cover: Foto ©ninafisch / pixelio.de

More available books at **www.hansebooks.com**

Yours aff
Eddie

MEMORIAL

OF

EDWARD C. D. LINES,

LATE

Captain of Co. C, 2d Reg't Kansas Cavalry.

———

NEW HAVEN:

Tuttle, Morehouse & Taylor, Printers.

1867.

"EDDIE," as he was familiarly called in the family circle, was born in New Haven, Conn., in May, 1836. His childhood and youth were marked by the same attractive traits of character that distinguished his maturer years. He was always a favorite in every circle with which he was in any way connected. His parents cannot recollect a single instance when, by any misconduct of his, they felt a pang or shed a tear. His whole life was specially marked in a preëminent degree by an unselfish, self-sacrificing spirit; and in this spirit, when the peril of the nation called upon the people to rally for its salvation, it may be truly said of him as of thousands of others,

> Thy life a willing sacrifice was given,
> Thy country's life to save.

To treasure up therefore in a permanent form, some suitable memorials of his "useful life and heroic death," these papers have been arranged and published. Unavoidable circumstances have occasioned protracted delay, but it is believed, nevertheless, that what should have been done at an earlier period may be wisely, appropriately and profitably done now. May we not hope that many of the young men of our day may find in these pages another incentive, to a higher and purer life.   C. B. L.

NOVEMBER, 1867.

ADDRESS BY REV. S. W. S. DUTTON, D. D..

AT THE FUNERAL OF CAPT. E. C. D. LINES.

We commemorate to-day, in sorrow yet with grateful pride and joy, another of the costly sacrifices laid upon the altar of patriotism, humanity and religion—a husband, a father, a son, a brother, in the flower of early manhood, freely offered, from a sense of duty to country, to righteousness and to God.

Such sacrifices are not in vain. They who offer them do more, perhaps, by their heroic death than they could do by their continued life. Though dead they speak, and all the more impressively and effectually because of their death. Yet in order to this influence of their example, it is necessary that their heroic service and sacrifice should be known. It is eminently proper, therefore, that on this occasion there should be given a brief account of the youthful patriot martyr, whose body, recovered from a far distant battle field, we are now to deposit in the cemetery of his native city.

The patriotism of Mr. Lines began to be signally manifested five years before the commencement of the present war, and was called out by the aggressions of that great iniquity which, long the chief cause of our national troubles, at length broke out in open rebellion. When the territory, pledged forever to freedom by the faith of the nation, in the "Missouri Compromise," as it was called, was open to slavery by the repeal of that compromise in what was named the "Kansas Nebraska Bill," it was seen that the only way to preserve that vast and fertile region to freedom, was to occupy it with such a number of freedom-loving citizens as would constitute a majority in the Territory, and so control the character of its institutions. Accordingly, patriotic men, in various parts of the country, and especially in New England, inspired by their own zeal for the interests of our country and humanity, and also by the zeal and aid of others, emigrated to that part of the country ; and, after a severe, protracted and sacrificing struggle with the unscrupulous and ruffianly bands, who from various parts of the slaveholding region, and especially from the neighboring counties of Missouri, invaded the Territory, and trampled on the rights of its real citizens, and assumed its civil control, they succeeded at length in rescuing Kansas from slavery, and making it a State more devoted, probably, to the interests of freedom than any other State in the Union. A noble work of righteousness and humanity—causing the first turning of the tide in favor of freedom ; a tide which has swept on and will sweep on till slavery is banished from the whole country.

In that movement, as is well known by those who hear me, the father of our departed friend, Mr. Charles B. Lines, who had occupied a prominent place of influence in this community, and especially in the Church and congregation worshiping in this Sanctuary, participated, being the leader in the formation of a company, which went out to Kansas and settled the town

of Wabaunsee. At that time, Edward, his second son, then
twenty years of age, though having a good position and fair
prospects here, expressed his earnest desire to be permitted to
take part in the enterprise. He joined the company, which
left us with the hearty approbation and Christian benediction
of a multitude here. Hardly had the colony become settled,
when the territory was invaded by armed bands of "Border
Ruffians," as they were appropriately termed, who murdered
men in their houses and fields, burned the new city of Lawrence, and were determined to lay waste the towns and cities
of the Free State citizens, and to control the elections and civil
affairs of the Territory in the interest of Slavery-extension.
At that time, a military company was organized in Wabaunsee
and vicinity, which marched at once to Lawrence. One of the
most active and influential in raising this company was Edward
Lines, who was chosen Lieutenant, and on the subsequent
illness of its Captain was much of the time its actual commander. This company, being armed in the most effectual
manner with Sharpe's rifles, (which, by the way, were raised
for them by subscription at a meeting in this very church, quite
unexpectedly indeed, in response to an incidental statement
during the progress of the meeting, that they had been disappointed in receiving, from another source, the necessary
weapons for their self-defence,) this company, thus constituted
and armed, was among the most efficient and self-sacrificing in
defending the Territory against the savage invasions of that
period, and in maintaining the rights of the Free-State
majority.

In that campaign, young Lines suffered severely from exposures and hardships, contracting a disease which disabled him for months, and nearly cost him his life. But it was a school of training for the future. In it he developed, in a remarkable degree, the qualities of a thorough and able military character—courage, coolness, sagacity, firmness, enterprise, and high appreciation of strict military principle and order, and determination both to regard and secure it.

When the war of the rebellion began, by the assault upon Fort Sumpter, in the Spring of 1861, and the President of the United States called, by Proclamation, for 75,000 troops for a service of three months, our young friend was the first man in the county in which he resided to volunteer. He enlisted in a company which was made up from citizens of three contiguous, sparsely settled counties. He entered the service as a private, but upon the occurence of a vacancy a few days after the company was organized, he was unanimously chosen lieutenant, the company having become a part of the 2d Regiment of Kansas Infantry, under command of Col. Robert B. Mitchell.

Here I will digress for a moment to refer to an event that occurred about three months before this, the remembrance of which is an unspeakable consolation to sorrowing hearts to-day—the public profession by Mr. Lines, of his faith in Christ and his devotion to His service. In January, 1861, he united himself to the Church in Wabaunsee, together with his wife. He had been trained, from childhood, in the nurture and admonition of the Lord, and had always been correct in his principles, pure and upright in his conduct, and thoughtful upon the themes of religion ; but had not before decided to take an open position on the Lord's side, in the way of His appointment. Thus he had the highest qualification for the perilous service upon which he was soon called to enter,—faith in Christ, the Savior of sinners, and faith in God, the God of Providence, the God of battles, the God of righteousness and grace. And so, when the war began he engaged in it as a soldier of Christ, as well as a soldier of his country.

His military merits were soon discovered and appreciated by Col. Mitchell, who, on account of the illness of his Adjutant, appointed him acting Adjutant. This position of acting Adjutant he held during that most trying summer campaign in Southwest Missouri, under the command of the heroic and lamented Gen. Lyon. In the various marches, skirmishes and battles of that campaign, he was very active, brave and efficient. In the severest of the fights, the fearfully contested battle of Wilson's Creek, in which Gen. Lyon fell, leading on his men against superior numbers, Mr. Lines was greatly exposed, riding hither and thither over the battle field to carry orders, and had early an increased responsibility, because both the colonels of the two Kansas Regiments, Col. Mitchell and Col. Dietzler, were wounded and borne off the field. Mr. Lines was in the van of the conflict, near Gen. Lyon when he was killed. His exposures and his remarkable preservation are seen in the facts, that his sword was struck, and severely marked by three rifle balls, his saddle was raked by a canister shot, two horses during the day were shot under him, and he was, towards the close, while on the retreat, struck on the shoulder with a piece of spent shell, which did him no harm beyond a lameness for a few days.

Col. Mitchell, afterwards, expressed to a friend the highest admiration of the courage, self-possession, efficiency, fidelity and thorough soldierly bearing of Mr. Lines, on that day of fearful fight. He said that he had been sending him with orders here and there over the field, in the face of musketry and cannonade, when, in one of the pauses of his work, Mr. Lines rode up to him, and said, "Don't feel any delicacy, Colonel ; send me anywhere you wish me to go."

His courage, and his humanity also, and self-forgetfulness, are seen in another fact, which occurred at the beginning of the retreat, after the death of Gen. Lyon. They were passing through groves of timber, in which shot and shell were cutting their way so thickly, that there was a continual dropping on them of leaves and twigs and branches, when he heard on one side the groaning of a boy. He went to him, and found he was one of the drummer boys, or one attached in some way to the musical service. Mr. Lines dismounted, placed the wounded boy upon his horse, and led him on, necessarily at a slow gait, till they were beyond the reach of the enemy.

Though the regiment originally enlisted on a call for three months service, yet through the influence of the patriotic Col. Mitchell, they served between four and five months. Soon after they were mustered out of service, in the autumn of 1861, they were organized anew as the 2d Regiment Kansas Cavalry ; and Mr. Lines was appointed 1st Lieut. of Co. C. In this position he served only a short time : his Col., Robert B. Mitchell, was soon after promoted to a Brigadier General, and appointed him as one of his Aids. Gen. Mitchell, with his brigade, was sent to join the Army of the Cumberland, on the east of the Missisippi. And in all the weary forced marches and severe engagements of that Army, in Kentucky and Tennessee, Mr. Lines endured bravely, and was entirely unharmed. In the desperate fought battle of Perryville, in which a part of our forces were allowed to contend against superior numbers, though reinforcements might easily have been brought up, Gen. Mitchell's brigade was in the thickest of the fight, and performed distinguished service. Such was the confidence of Gen. Mitchell in Mr. Lines, that he was accustomed to ask him to perform many duties of a responsible and critical nature, which perhaps did not strictly belong to him but to other officers. And the General used to give his reason in such language as this, when he had sent him, for example, to station pickets at night, a service not pertaining to his office :—"When I know you have stationed the pickets, I can sleep." Indeed, such was his over-work in consequence of the confidence reposed in him by his General, and his own desire to do all in his power, that he felt it necessary to resign his position as Aid, and request to be returned to his old Company, in the 2d Kansas Cavalry. This was in November, 1862. His Company, hearing that he was about to return to them, unanimously recommended him to be appointed to the office of Captain, which was then vacant ; and he was accordingly appointed. In this position he remained, sharing in all the severe service of that Regiment during the remainder of 1862, and the Spring and Summer of 1863.

His position as Captain was one of peculiar exposure; for on account of the confidence of the Commander in him, and his well disciplined Company, that Company was selected as the advance guard of the Brigade Command, a place of special danger in a country where the enemy is accustomed to the practice of ambush. And it was Capt. Lines' custom always to ride in front of his Company, because he thought it his duty so to do. He used to say to his father, when exhorting him not to expose himself unnecessarily:—"Do not give yourself any uneasiness about me. I shall not risk any unnecessary exposures, and on the other hand, I shall always endeavor to be just where my duty calls me."

It was in the performance of this duty, leading his Company as an advance guard, that he lost his life by a volley from a party of the enemy in ambush, a few miles from Fort Smith, Arkansas.

The account of this, I will give in the language of an eye-witness, the Surgeon of the Regiment, Doct. J. P. Root, formerly Lieut. Gov. of the State of Kansas, and one of the original Wabaunsee Colony, addressed by him in a letter to Capt. Lines' bereaved wife. He says:

"Long ere this reaches you, you will have learned of the death of your dear husband, whose remains we have this day buried in the U. S. Cemetery, at Fort Smith; the members of the Kansas Cavalry, standing as tearful mourners around his grave, as with military honors we bade adieu to the body, that so recently contained the spirit of the brave, noble, high-minded, gallant and lovely officer, who by heroic deeds in his country's service, as well as private acts in social life, had endeared himself to all who knew him.

In our recent campaign of several weeks of almost constant forced marches by night and day, Col. Cloud had selected your husband's company as his special body-guard for his brigade command—a deserved compliment to the bravery and integrity of Capt. Lines, and his gallant company.

During most of our recent marches, extending a distance of nearly five-hundred miles, through Southwestern Missouri, Northwestern and Western Arkansas, both above and below the Arkansas River, through the Cherokee Indian Nation, to Fort Gibson, through the Creek and Choctaw Nation, well on to Texas, constantly chasing rebels of every grade, from the bushwhacking assassin bandit, to the rebel who dared to stand behind his cannon, and contend for his ground, until put to flight by our surer aim and sterner purpose, Capt. Lines was most of the time in our advance.

We had chased Gen. Steele and Cooper nearly to Texas without getting a general engagement with the enemy, and had turned back towards Fort Smith, where we expected a battle with Gen. Caball. In this, however, we were disappointed ; for the cowardly traitor left our front during the night ; and the next day, Gen. Blunt ordered Col. Cloud, with a portion of his Cavalry and Artillery, to pursue. This order was promptly obeyed. When about twenty miles south of this place (Fort Smith) we overtook the enemy and engaged him, strongly posted among the mountains, immediately upon what is called the Back-bone—a high ridge of rocky and timbered

land.   The battle was opened by a volley of musketry, nearly
in our faces, from a company in ambush.   Capt. Lines' company was in the advance and received the first shock, at which
your husband received a fatal wound from a rifle ball.

Capt. Lines fell while gallantly leading his men, at the head
of our column.   I was riding with Col. Cloud, close behind,
and immediately went to the Captain's assistance.   But all I
could do was to alleviate.   With a smile he said to me :
' Doctor, I am mortally wounded.   I have felt all the time that
I should not survive this Campaign.   I do not fear death.
How sad my wife, my father and friends will feel !   This is all
that troubles me.'   He cheered his wounded comrades who were
groaning around him ;   but not a groan or murmur escaped his
lips.   He desired me to tell you and his father and his friends,
how he died.   Never did bravery show itself more than when
with heroic fortitude he bore his most excruciating pains without a sigh of sadness, while the groans of the wounded were on
all sides, and the shot and shell of the enemy were falling thick
around us.   *   *   *   He lived between three and four hours,
long enough to be cheered by the knowledge that the enemy
had been routed completely, and had hurried from the field,
leaving their dead and dying in our hands.

What can I say to cheer your widowed heart ?   When danger
threatened Kansas in its early history, your husband gave
himself to her defence.   Never can I forget those scenes in
which I knew him so well.   When the present rebellion first
broke out, he again sprang forward to rescue his country, and
foremost on many a hard fought field has he testified his gallant

patriotism and undying devotion to the cause of freedom. A shower of leaden hail has been falling around him since, as Adjutant of the 2d Regiment of Kansas Volunteers, in the Wilson's Creek battle, he fought close beside the lamented Lyon, up to the hour when he lost his life at the battle of the Back-bone.

I knew him well, and dearly did I love the brave, good young man. All loved him. He has left a host of friends, both in military and civil life, who will ever cherish the memory of Capt. E. C. D. Lines."

A few additional particulars are given in a letter from J. W. Robinson, also a Surgeon of the 2d Kansas Regiment. He says: "Mr. Lines was aware he should live but a few hours, and said that he died where he preferred to die—at the head of his Company. He had always tried (he said) to do his duty to his country, and he only regretted that he had not been able to do more." He died, Dr. Robinson adds, firmly believing in his better estate in the world to come.

Of the great respect and affection with which he was regarded, there is abounding testimony. Dr. Robinson says, "No man was ever more beloved by his company than he was; and no man more properly deserved it." He adds, that they were "almost frantic with grief" at his death.

The Manhattan Independent, published near his home, says, "We honored him for his self-sacrificing patriotism. He saw the liberties of his country imperilled, and he only thought of how he could devote a brave heart and an earnest life to her cause. He was the first man in his county to enlist. ✿ ✿ ✿

While Kansas has a history, his name will be mentioned as one of her most honored sons; one of the martyrs to the cause of liberty, whose fame, though pure and spotless now, will shine with increased lustre as the ages roll on."

The Union, published at Fort Smith, Arkansas, where his body was buried, says of him, "Never, since our connection with the army, has the fate of a man created a wider and more heartfelt sorrow; never was the sacrifice of one's life for his country made more bravely and seemingly more cheerfully."

The spirit which actuated him in entering and continuing in his country's service, is well expressed in his own language, in a letter to his wife, then in this part of the country. It was written after his first period of service, subsequent to the battle of Wilson's Creek, and just upon his enlisting again for three years or during the war—a dark hour in our country's history. He says, "I have sometimes thought that I would retire from my country's service to my home and family. But I know it would be wrong, and that you would love me less for deserting my country in this dark and trying hour. Lives must be given up, riches and all man possesses must be cast aside, and our country's flag kept waving. I thank God every day of my life, that my arm is kept strong to battle against our country's enemies. And it is a wonder to me, that so many of our country's young men should persist in remaining inactive, and allow for one moment a doubt as it regards our success."

And then in his last letter, written just before the battle in which he lost his life, and evidently tinged with the feeling which he expressed to Dr. Root, when he said, "I have felt all the time that I should not survive this campaign," he remarks, "we are expecting a battle, and I write this knowing it is possible that this may be my last letter to you. But I hope that God will spare my life for your sake. If I should be killed, you will have the satisfaction of knowing that I died with my face to the enemies of our country, and in its defence. May God watch over you, and bless you! If I die, think that it is God's will. And do not give up, but live as happy as you can, and teach our sweet child to love the memory of its father."

His motive in all his military career was not personal ambition, but pure and earnest patriotism, and a sense of duty to God and the cause of righteousness and humanity.

And now, in conclusion, need a word be said to commend his example to us, especially to the young men, many of whom have known him—his example of patriotism, of purity, of courage, of self-sacrificing devotion to the right, and especially of faith in Christ and fidelity in his service.

We mourn that his life was so short. But it was not short, if we measure it by deeds and services instead of years. And his example will inspire many to be like him, and to fill more than one place like his. Then we know that he died in the Lord's time, and we have been taught by our friend's exhortation, as well as by the principles of piety, to say, "Thy will be done." And assured of his interest in Him who is the resurrection and the life, we may well rejoice in our loss as his infinite gain.

With such thoughts we may adopt the words of the sacred poet, in our last address to him whose body we are now to consign to the grave :

"Go to the grave in all thy glorious prime,
   In full activity of zeal and power;
Thou art not called away before thy time ;—
   The Lord's appointment is the servant's hour.

Go to the grave ; at noon from labor cease ;
   Rest on thy sheaves, thy harvest-task is done :
Come from the heat of battle, and in peace,
   Soldier, go home ; with thee the fight is won.

Go to the grave; for there thy Savior lay
   In death's embrace, ere He rose on high ;
And all the ransomed, by that narrow way,
   Pass to eternal life beyond the sky.

Go to the grave :—no; take thy seat above;
   Be thy pure spirit present with the Lord,
Where thou for faith and hope hast perfect love,
   And open vision for the written word."

LETTER FROM GEN. MITCHELL.

EXTRACT FROM A LETTER WRITTEN BY GEN. ROBT. B. MITCHELL,
TO THE FATHER OF CAPTAIN LINES, JUNE 11, 1864.

Upon the organization of the Second Kansas Regiment in May, 1861, under my command, I found your son, an officer, in one of the companies.

The conviction formed from the slight acquaintance I had with him prior to his entrance into service, that he would demonstrate the possession of peculiar abilities as an officer, induced me to observe him carefully in the discharge of his official duties.

I found him apt to learn the minutiæ of such duty, prompt and correct in its application, and while rigid in the require- ment of the performance of every duty by the men under his command, yet, by his kindness and care for them, the respect enforced by his position and commands, was accompanied by a deep, earnest and soldierly affection on the part of the men of his company. In his associations with his brother officers, his high-toned bearing and conversation, his geniality of manner, his knowledge of his new profession, his correct and conscientious performance of duty, and his considerate regard for the feelings of others, under the most irritating of circumstances, made him universally loved, admired and respected.

3

Upon the long and weary march in Missouri, immediately following the muster into service of the regiment, when those young troops—almost entirely unsupplied with the essentials to a soldier's comfort, and when inexperience made such lack more difficult to be borne—executed marches and endured privations almost unequalled before or since by veteran soldiers, his cheering voice was constantly heard encouraging the weary, his hand was extended to help the wayside fallen, and despite his delicate frame, by the strong purpose consequent upon his conviction of the necessity for the sake of others of remaining at his post, he bore up against all hardships, and in the most gloomy periods, when fatigue, exhaustion, lack of food and of sleep, tended to dispirit all, he, supported by a conviction of duty to be done, and by the dictates of that kindness that induced so large a forgetfulness of self, unmindful of his own safety, his health, or his comfort, devoted himself to the task of restoring confidence and strength to the weary and disabled for new exertions; all this was done by him without orders or direction, and while he was unaware that his conduct was the subject of observation or commendation by his superior officers, who recognized the great and faithful services rendered by him at the time.

In the affairs at Forsyth and Dug Springs, his conduct was marked by distinguished gallantry.

The illness of my Adjutant, Lieut. Thompson, enforced his absence from duty, and Lieut. Lines was detailed to perform the duties of Adjutant, in his stead.

Lieut. Lines brought to the performance of the multifarious, constant and arduous duties of the position of Adjutant, the same urbanity and conscientiousness in the discharge of duty, that had characterized him as a company officer, together with an amount of administrative ability that won from all the warmest encomiums.

In this position, the relation he bore to me was of an exceedingly confidential nature, and the ease with which he comprehended all plans, issued the necessary orders for their execution, and superintended the details of such execution, the aptness of his suggestions and his undirected action, all demonstrated to me the possession of talent of an unusually high order, and induced me to regard him rather as a friend and adviser, than as a junior officer.

Upon the field at Wilson's Creek, where the long, weary campaign of 1861 culminated in that heroic struggle of the lamented Lyon, against an enemy five times the number of his little band, the gallantry and efficiency of your son were particularly conspicuous, and did much to inspire the regiment with the spirit that enabled them to withstand and beat back the successive charges of an enemy so much exceeding them in number. From the nature of the duties attendant upon his position as Adjutant, he was very much exposed to the enemy's fire ; but he rode unscathed and erect wherever his presence could be of service, his clarion voice shouting words of encourgement or direction, or when the stern duties of the day permitted, speaking words of solace and comfort to the stricken. Among the brave men upon that field he will ever be remembered by those who saw him as among the first and bravest.

I was left wounded at Springfield, Mo., subsequent to that engagement, while the regiment proceeded to Fort Leavenworth, having an engagement with the rebels at Shelbina, Mo., while en route.

In the labors consequent upon the muster-out of the regiment at Fort Leavenworth, 1862, prior to its re-organization, the knowledge of the practice of the army, and its routine of official transactions and papers, which Lieut. Lines acquired with great facility and applied with great exactness, tended much to expedite the formation of the new organization.

During the winter of 1861–2, I was in almost constant, daily intercourse with him in Washington, and the affection and respect that his conduct in the field had won, was strengthened by new developments of his possession of great social charms, eminent purity and honesty of character, and a quickness of perception and depth of understanding, that made his facile conversation and geniality of manner doubly attractive.

Upon assuming command of a Brigade, I detailed him upon my personal staff as an Aide-de-Camp, in which capacity he was with me from May, 1862, until October, of the same year.

With my command he proceeded from Fort Riley, Kansas, to Corinth, Mississippi, thence to join the army of Maj. Gen. Buell, at Nashville, Tennessee. He was with me in the Kentucky campaign in the summer of 1862, and participated in the engagement at Perryville, and at Lancaster, Kentucky, in that campaign.

During this period, I had frequent occasion to call upon him for the performance of duties of danger and importance, and I was always well assured that if knowledge of his profession, energy, endurance and conscientiousness could accomplish the task set before him, it would be done.

At the conclusion of the Kentucky campaign in October, 1862, Lieut. Lines returned with me to Kansas, and there yielding to the solicitations of his friends and his own conviction, that he could be of greater service with his regiment,—then I think in Arkansas,—he returned to duty with it.

I urged him also to take this step, despite my disinclination to lose so valuable an officer, so honorable a gentleman, and so true a friend, from my staff, because I believed that in the line of his regiment, he could more readily obtain that promotion that his long, valuable and faithful services and his eminent fitness for high rank demanded, than he could in the staff corps. Justice to him, the service, the cause, and the country, demanded this personal sacrifice at my hands.

His new field of duty being widely separated from my own, I heard but seldom from him, but always that his career was marked with those honorable and soldierly qualities that had always been attendant upon his actions.

One letter informed me of his promotion, and the commencement, as I believed and hoped, of a series of rewards, in more and more advanced grades of rank ; and the next that I received bringing any news of his regiment, told the sad story that he had fallen.

The intelligence came at the evening of one of the days of the hard fought battle of Chicamauga. With the din of the cannon still ringing in our ears, with the occasional shot that told of the vigilant sentinels' watch of the movements of the enemy, with whom the next day we were again to struggle, with the groans of the wounded and dying ascending in our hearing, we who had known and served with your son, forgot for a time, the terrible business and incidents of the day, and were called upon to join with our sorrow for those who had that day fallen by our side, tears for the memory of our friend, our comrade, our brother officer, who had met a soldier's fate on a far distant field.

Tired, weary and worn, with the dust of battle still on our faces, those who had known "Ed Lines" sorrowed for his untimely death, and recalled with melancholy pleasure the many instances of courage, gentleness and kindness, with which association with him was so fraught.

But he is gone ; you have lost a good and affectionate son, the cause has lost an able and a brave soldier, the country a patriot, and we, his associates, have lost a true and well tried friend.

May we not hope that the story of his upright life and glorious death, told by some appreciative and able tongue, will furnish a bright exemplar to which you, the father of so good, so noble, so pure a son, may see other fathers pointing their offspring as a model for a true and perfect life.

With assurances of my condolence in your great bereavement, I am very truly,

Your obedient servant,

ROBT. B. MITCHELL,

Brig. General.

APPENDIX.

Captain LINES was very affectionate toward his family and friends, and unusually thoughtful of them, especially in writing whenever it was possible. A few extracts from the hundreds of letters received from him, are given below, which indicate the current of his thoughts and the character of the man:—

Extracts from letters to his wife, when first entering the Army.

"You must remember there will be a great number of "Eddies" in this war, and some of them must die before our country is again quiet, and if God sees fit that I should be one to surrender my life for my country's good, I shall not complain; pray and trust in God; He rules every thing for good.

We are going South with Gen. Mitchell; "duty calls me to active life—and I expect to see within the next few weeks, many a noble man die a soldier's death and fill a soldier's grave. I trust Eddie will be spared; it is hard to think that many kind husbands are leaving their dear ones for the last time, and at the boats this eve, it was hard to see the wives taking a farewell kiss of many a brave and noble man, for some must die."

WABAUNSEE, KANSAS,
October 8th, 1861.

DEAREST AND BELOVED KITTIE,

I arrived in Wabaunsee Saturday evening. They were all glad to see me. Our dear brother Elsworth, I found to be in a dying state; he knew me but said but little. You can imagine how I felt, coming home after such a trip to spend a few days with those I love, to find one of them so near the other world. He died last night and was willing to go; his trust was in God. It is a hard blow to us all. But father and mother were so much relieved to know that he had put his trust in the Lord. Dearest Kittie, this is a hard blow for me, I so little expected to find one so loved to be taken from us. I have looked to such a pleasant visit, and to find all so changed, it makes me feel as I never felt before. But it is God's will and I submit. I know it will be hard to go away and part with father and mother; it seems as if it would be a last and a long farewell. But I think it a duty I owe my God and my country. If Kittie were here, it seems to me that I could not again part. But it may be for the best; Elsworth dead, Kittie miles away, and all looks so dark, it seems that I am no longer that Eddie of old, but a soldier whose life is one of trial and hardships, and but a step from the other world. It is hard thus to reflect, but I can not help it, and we must look at it just as it is, and be prepared for the worst. As I looked at our dear one this morning, cold in death, I could but feel that I should soon follow him to the Happy Land. I have for some time felt that death was not far off, and now it almost stares me in the face. But I fear not; in God I trust, and it makes me happy when I know that Kittie will submit to His will. Dearest and much loved one, could I but see you once again I would be so happy, and if it is possible for me to get to you, I shall try my best so to do.

PLANTER'S HOUSE, LEAVENWORTH, KANSAS, }
May 28th, 1862. }

DEAR FATHER.

I have but a few moments to write, as it is now after eleven o'clock, and I am quite tired. We have had a review to-day, by Blunt, of the troops ordered to Tenn., and this afternoon and evening we have been shipping troops, and I am tired out. We start to-morrow at noon. I go with the expectation of seeing some hard fighting, and knowing that I may be one of the Kansas men that will not come back. But it is all right; duty calls and I am ready and willing to take my chances. From the news we get now it looks dark for our troops, and some think that we will be ordered from St. Louis to Washington. I care not, if we can only do some good I hope that you will write to my dear wife often, and in case I should fall, do what you can to make her happy. I will write as often as I can, and tell you all. But I feel confident that I will come out all right.

Ever your loving son, ED.

IN CAMP NEAR MURFREESBORO, TENN., }
September 3d, 1862. }

DEAR FATHER.

I have but a few moments to write. I am quite well,—never better in my life. We are on the march for Nashville, Tenn. It is very hot, and we have warm work before us. I think it is about even with the North and South. It looks dark for us. Direct your letters to me, at Nashville, Tenn., care Gen. R. B. Mitchell. My love to all.—In haste. Your affectionate son, ED.

BATTLE GROUND, NEAR PERRYVILLE, KY., }
October 10th, 1862. }

DEAR FATHER.

We have just finished a big battle. I am unhurt.—None of Gen.'s staff are injured. We have lost, of our command, (Mitchell's alone), 500,—our whole loss is yet unknown. I am satisfied with our success; but for three days and nights having been in the saddle; hungry and worn out, I cannot write. We have all of our dead (as well as theirs) yet to bury. I have lost some good friends in this fight. I will write in a few days. My love to all. Our Wabaunsee boys are all well. In haste. Your affectionate son, ED.

———————

HEAD-QUARTERS, S. W DIST., SPRINGFIELD, MO., }
March 12th, 1863. }

DEAR FATHER.

I am quite well, and have all I want to do. I am engaged now in hunting Horse Thieves. Caught two Saturday night, and got seven head of Stock; and five to-day. The Boys are all well. I will write you a letter in a few days. I am expecting a letter from you. My love to all. I hope that mother is well.

Your dear son, ED.

———————

After his last visit, in speaking of his babe, he writes:

"Our married life has been so pleasant, I can and do think of it every day as a bright spot in my life. I hope God in His goodness, will spare us to each other, and that long years of happiness are in store for us. I will be careful and hopeful; how dearly, fondly I love our sweet babe; I trust she may be spared to us. God has been so kind in giving us such a treasure; can we ever thank Him as we should. May God bless and protect her, and give you strength to bear with her, and bring her up as we both so much wish to. 'I feel so happy that I have seen her and pressed her to my heart.'"

———————

His last letter to his father.

NEAR CINCINNATI, ARK.
IN THE FIELD AND ON THE MARCH TO FORT GIBSON, }
August 19th, 1863. }

DEAR FATHER.

We have just stopped here for a few moments; we are on a forced march to join Gen. Blunt, at Gibson. We have had a hard trip since we left Cassville, but of this hereafter. I will only say that I have had the advance, and we have done some good work. We expect some hard fighting, and if I should be killed, I want you to settle up my business. I have Pay due me from July 1st, and Kittie will be entitled to a Pension. I would like to have it attended to at once. I fear not to die, but tremble to think of the effect it would have upon my dear wife and little one; but God rules and I trust all to Him. You will hear, as soon as the battle is over, of me, and, either dead or alive, it shall be a good account; I have brave men, and we will do good work. I can't write more, I have so much to do. If I fall, my papers will be sent to you. My love to all.

In much haste, your affectionate son, ED.

———————

FORT SMITH, ARK., }
September 2d, 1862. }

C. B. LINES, Esq.

Dear Sir,—I take my pen to perform one of the most melancholy duties of my life. I must acquaint you of the death of our beloved comrade in arms, and your dutiful and brave boy, Edward (Capt.) Lines, of Company C, of 2d Kansas Cavalry.

4

On the 8th day of August we left Springfield, to reinforce Gen. Blunt, then at Fort Gibson. We have been on a forced march nearly ever since that time. We found the enemy at Briertown or Brierville, in the Cherokee Nation, four days after leaving Fort Gibson; drove them to Perryville, near the Texas line, and burned the town; then we started for Fort Smith. Gen. Caball, with about 2,500 men, undertook to dispute our passage, but finally, after throwing a few shell at us from two howitzers, run. Our command, under Col. Cloud, marched about 17 miles, and were ambushed by the rebels, Company "C" being in our advance. The enemy formed in a dense growth of small timber and brush, and when our scouts came up, they let them pass through without firing a gun, but when Company C came up, they opened upon them a very heavy volley of infantry in two columns.

Your son was killed at that time. He was in the extreme advance, (as was his custom,) and was shot by a minnie ball, through the bowels and liver. He lived about 2½ or 3 hours after the wound, remaining entirely sensible to the last moment. He died as brave a man as ever gave his life for his country. Not a murmur or complaint escaped his lips. He said he should live but a few hours, and that he died where he preferred to die, at the head of his Company, firmly believing he would be better off in the world to come, and sending his warmest love to his wife, and father, and mother, and all his dear friends.

I cannot write as I would, I am so pained at the loss of Eddie; his Company are almost frantic with grief. I had no idea he was so beloved, except by myself! My heart is too full to write more.

Yours, in affliction,   J. W. R.,
Ass't Surgeon 2d Kansas Cavalry.

FORT SMITH, ARK.,
Aug. 3d, 1863.

CHAS. B. LINES, ESQ.,

Dear Sir:—With feelings of keenest sorrow I write you a brief account of the wounding and death of your dear son, my dear friend, and one of the bravest and best officers that have ever given their lives to their country. Capt. Lines' Company was made Col. Cloud's "body guard" for his Brigade command, when we left Springfield, and on all our forced marches, for several hundred miles, has been in the advance.

For nearly five hundred miles of almost uninterrupted forced marching, we have had nearly a continuous fight, chasing bushwhackers and rebels of every grade, skirmishing by day and skirmishing by night. Near Fort Smith, Col. Cloud's command was divided, a portion coming to the Fort with Gen. Blunt, and the remainder taking the southern road after the fleeing Gen. Caball. Tired as we all were, we overtook the rebels about twenty miles from Ft. Smith, strongly posted in the mountains, in one of the strongest natural positions for defence I have ever seen. Previous to the final engagement we were skirmishing with pickets, rear guards, &c., until your son boldly pushed forward with his brave boys, met almost at the muzzles of their guns the deadly discharge of over two hundred rifles, muskets, &c. Capt. Lines received a wound from a rifle ball, the ball entering the abdomen a little to the right of the centre and passing out beneath the ribs on the left side of the body. The intestines were wounded, and several small vessels were severed, causing slow but fatal hemorrhage. I was immediately with the Capt. as he fell from his wounded horse, and never have I seen more nobleness of spirit, more unflinching coolness and bravery displayed, than was exhibited during the last hours of your son's life; his cheerfulness was wonderful, notwithstanding his pains were extreme; he murmured not—not even a groan escaped his lips. From the first, he was fully aware of his critical condition, and that he could not recover. He often spoke of you and of his own little family. The leaving of his friends being his only regret—of them he spoke freely. He had an affectionate spirit, he loved and in return was beloved by a host of good and brave men, who will ever remember Capt. Lines with feelings of pure respect and esteem. I wish I could say something that might relieve the poignancy of your grief. I can only point to the God you worship, for comfort, and pray that we all may be prepared for our final departure, whether it shall be amid the din and smoke of battle, as dies the noble brave, or with our loving families in peaceful homes.

I have written in great haste, having a thousand things on hand. Please accept my heartiest sympathy, and believe me, as ever, your true friend.

J. P. R.,
Surgeon 2d Kan. Cavalry.

Extracts from a few of the many letters received by his family, after the death of Capt. Lines.

LAWRENCE, KANSAS,
October 2d, 1863.

DEAR SIR AND FRIEND.

You do not, I trust, need telling, that in your terrible loss—which we count our own—we all deeply sympathize. At such a time, as one says of one in similar circumstances:—"the poor common words of sympathy seem such a very mockery." I need not here repeat them. Nor is the road to "The Comforter" one so untraveled by you in the past, that in this new affliction you need a guide to the presence of that friend. You have so often proved his faithfulness, that you are, with the Psalmist, fully prepared to say, "Even the night shall be light about me." —"Thy rod and thy staff they comfort me." I feel that our *Churches* have been smitten in the loss of one, of whom, though often mentioned in my hearing during my long journeyings, I have yet heard no word but as in his favor as a soldier and man. Need I say more to you, to his mother, his wife or of him.

What you deem the best obituary notice published, with any added particulars, from your pen, we would crave for permanent preservation in our "Record" of Kansas Churches.

Your friend and younger brother, L. B.

C. B. LINES, Esq.

LAWRENCE, KANSAS,
March 9th, 1864.

Hon. C. B. LINES.

Dear Sir:—You have received a heavy blow, but it does not fall alone upon you. I feel that I have cause to mourn the loss of a dear friend in your noble hearted son, and the State has lost a treasure not easily replaced. Please accept my heart-felt sympathy in this affliction.

Very truly, your friend,   C. R.

NEW YORK,
October 16th, 1863.

MY DEAR FRIEND.

I have just received notice of the death of your son. I must say, in view of the facts of his death and of your well grounded hope of his preparation for the change, that I feel like offering you my congratulation rather than any ordinary expressions of condolence. It is a *great* thing for a man to give a son to die as he died, in the assurance of hope for the hereafter. He will live in the affections of all his family for *generations;* his deeds of valor and sacrifice will be told at the fire-sides of your children's children, for centuries, and the fact and glory of dying for his country is inseparably connected with his name for all time. Do not mourn for him! Thank God rather that you had such a son, and that he gave himself so nobly to the cause of right and liberty.

Yours truly,   S. B. C.

Mr. C. B. LINES.

SPRINGFIELD, MISSOURI,
September 19th, 1863.

DEAR SIR.

The news lately received of the death of your son, Capt. Lines, is sad. It brings to me the intelligence that I have lost a firm and true friend, a brave and gallant officer, while to you it conveys the information that you have lost a son who was an honor to his parents. It was not my fortune to be with him on that day, but knowing him as I did, I feel proud to learn that he died nobly, that he was stricken down while in the discharge of his duty to his country, and he died, as he had lived, loved and honored by all who knew him. I sincerely sympathize with you in this affliction.

Respectfully,   O. A. B., Lt. Col. 2d Kan. Cav.

C. B. LINES, Esq., Topeka, Kansas.

LAWRENCE, KANSAS,
December 8th, 1863.

Hon. C. B. LINES.

Dear Sir:—Now that the first inevitable pang has been assuaged by time, will I obtrude upon the sanctity of your grief, if I assure you how much I sympathize with you in the loss of your son Edward. Although a comparative stranger to you, I could class *him* as one of my valued friends. During my connection with the Second Regiment, I had many opportunities to learn and admire his many good qualities, and to know that to many beside myself he endeared himself. Beside your personal loss, the State has lost a gallant soldier and honest gentleman. Will you consider me one who knew his worth and lament his loss.

I am, very dear sir, yours respectfully,   E. D. T.

NEW HAVEN, CONN.,
 October 24th, 1863.

MY DEAR FRIEND.

I need not assure you that I was deeply affected when the news came that Edward had fallen. The loss of such a young man, to his family, to his parents, and to society, it is painful to think of. What ties are broken,—what fond anticipations destroyed,—what hopes crushed. But when we look at *life* as it is—but a brief speck in the whole of man's existence—what matter is it so far as the individual is concerned, whether it is terminated a few years sooner or later. To man the only question of importance is: has the life, whether longer or shorter, been what life should be. And oh, how well does your son's record answer this question. To family and friends the death of one so loved, and so apparently needed by them, is a great affliction; and to human vision an irreparable loss. But faith can look beyond the present appearance and trust in a Heavenly Father who looks beyond the present, even to the end, and orders all things well,—making "all things work together for good to those who love God." And then what cause you have to rejoice that your son has been taken *in the fullness of honors*, and placed beyond the possible danger or fear of failure. Your dear son has secured what but few ever attain in this world—his name will go down in history as one of the martyrs for liberty and freedom,—with the Warrens and Hales of the Revolution; and the Lyons, the Russells and the Blakes, that Connecticut has given to their country in this war.

Hoping to see you again in the flesh, and earnestly praying for God's blessings to rest upon you and all near and dear to you.

I am, Truly yours,   S. D. P.

LAWRENCE, KANSAS,
 Nov., 1863.

DEAR SIR:—

I heard of the death of your son with deep sorrow. Honored and good, he has been cut down in the spring of life, and has gone where the tumult of battle will never molest him. Perhaps your son never *fully* realized the weighty issues that are staked upon the result of this war; but I knew him well enough to be sure that he did not fight for pay, or glory, merely. Our dear Lord, who gave His life to save a *world*, will welcome with unutterable love one who fell in the effort to lift and save a *race*. In His arms you can leave your boy with the assurance that it is well with him. And if at times you feel that your son is lost to you, try to comfort yourself with the thought that he may be nearer to you now, and more helpful, than when he was on the plains of Arkansas.

I pray that you will accept my deep sympathy for you in this bereavement. The event will not have happened in vain, if it brings you nearer to that cross where alone is rest.   Most truly,   H. M. S.

Letter from his former Teacher.

NEW HAVEN, CONN.,
November, 1st, 1867.

Hon. CHARLES B. LINES.

Dear Sir:—I am glad to learn that you are about to publish a memoir of your son, Edward, who gave his life for his country during the recent rebellion. His noble record should be preserved, because we instinctively feel that the memory of such a man should not perish, as well as because we want to spread and perpetuate the influence of his example.

His was a great contribution to the vast sum of noble acts by which our country has been saved for liberty, and liberty for the world. But beyond even this, we are brought to honor our common human nature more by these instances of heroism and devotion, that show us what lies dormant and concealed in it, until some stirring call brings it out to the sight of men.

The thought that the quiet, unassuming lad, who sat before me among his hundred and fifty schoolmates, has been in counsel and in action all that your son was, heightens to me the value of those who occupy their seats now. I see the possibilities that lie undeveloped, and feel that my work is ennobled by them. And not students merely, but men everywhere, at the plough, in the workshop, are more now to us than they were some years ago. Their thoughts, their rights, their dignity weigh more in our estimation. Grateful as we are to those who fell in this war, we have not yet learned to appreciate fully their influence on the present as on all the future.

> " They died in giving [us]
> Liberty; but left a deathless lesson,—
> A name which is a virtue; and a soul
> Which multiplies itself throughout all time."

Your son for years sat before me, as I sat where I am now writing. As my eye at this moment falls upon his seat and desk, I recall him perfectly; quiet, unassuming, studious, eminently trusted to do his duty at all times, honored and loved by all who knew him; what else should we have looked for but a life, however long or short, filled out with duty performed. How blind were we not to see in him all this surety for his future. The old Spartans went into battle with their crowns already on their heads. There was that in them which ensured victory even in defeat. If our eyes had been opened as those of a prophet of old, we should have seen him even in his boyhood thus crowned for life by his virtues, his firmness under temptation, and that perseverance in the right which was the insurance of his success. You have not ceased to grieve, you never will, for the loss to you of solace, of aid and reliance, as life grows old; but your grief is lightened by the thought that he wielded just the sword that our Lord came to bring; that your loss has brought gain to the world and to him, too, in that kingdom of God for the bringing on of which it really was, that he laid down his life.

Very truly yours,   W. H. R.

A FEW EXTRACTS FROM THE PRESS.

The Late Captain Lines.

A letter to the Commercial Advertiser, contains the following particulars of his fall:

" As Cloud's advanced guard, led by Captain Lines, approached, the rebels fired, and he fell from his horse, shot through the bowels. The ball entered his loins on the left side and passed entirely through his body, coming out near the right hip. He survived about four hours. In death his face wore the same expression of constant courage, and of calm and dauntless energy, that marked it in the discharge of all his duties, in camp and battle."

The funeral of the late Capt. E. C. D. Lines, will be attended at the North Church on Thursday, at 4 o'clock, P. M.

Captain Lines was killed on the 1st of September last, in the Indian country, near Arkansas, and temporarily buried at Fort Smith. He was advancing upon the enemy, at the head of his column, through a deeply wooded and rough country, his company constituting the advance guard of the brigade, under Col Cloud. They were ambushed by the rebels, who rose as they approached, and fired a deadly volley. Capt. Lines fell mortally wounded, and died in three hours.

His remains have been brought to his native city in care of his father, for interment, in compliance with his dying request, and the earnest desire of his deeply afflicted widow, who is now permanently located in this vicinity.

We quote from the " Fort Smith Union," a loyal paper, issued at Fort Smith, under date of September 2d, the following extract:—" Seldom in the history of this cruel, unnatural rebellion, have we been called upon to perform a more painful duty than to record the death of this brave young officer. Never, since our connection with the army, has the fate of a man created a wider and more heartfelt sorrow; never was the sacrifice of one's life made more bravely and seemingly more cheerfully." He died peacefully, and in hope of a glorious resurrection.—*New Haven Courier.*

Captain Lines was a native of Connecticut, in which State he received his early education, and made his home, until the commencement of troubles in Kansas. He came to that young territory with his father and brother, together with a large and respectable number of old friends, and formed the beautiful little town of Waubonsee, on the Kansas river. When the ballot-box was trampled under foot by an invading foreign force, and Free State men were murdered in their own houses and fields, Captain Lines was one of the first to resist tyranny and form a company for the protection of the people, of which he was elected Lieutenant, being then scarcely twenty-one years old. This was, probably, the first Sharp's rifle company in Kansas. He was in many of the fights and skirmishes during the trying times of '56.

As soon as the South signified her determination to sever the Union, by firing upon Fort Sumpter, Captain Lines was the first man from his county to offer his services to his country. He entered the army in 1861 as a private, but was elected and appointed a Lieutenant. The first important engagement in which he took a part, was the battle of Wilson's Creek, where he acted as Adjutant to the old Kansas Second. He was in all the actions which occurred in Missouri and Arkansas, until Col. Mitheell was promoted to a Brigadier, when he was placed upon his staff and sent to the trans-Mississippi army. Here he served with distinguished honor to himself and his country, and went through all those weary forced marches and desperate engagements without receiving a wound. Last autumn he was transferred to the Kansas Second again, and promoted soon after to a Captaincy.

On the 1st of September, Gen. Blunt had ordered Col. Cloud to pursue Cabell's retreating army. Captain Lines company formed the advance, and were ambushed. The enemy were so hard pursued, they were compelled to make a stand, and a heavy volley was fired from a cornfield at the head of our column. Capt. L. fell mortally wounded, and lived about three hours. He seemed as cheerful after his wound as before, encouraging his men to do their duty. He said he had but two regrets, one dying away from his friends, and the other that he had not been able to do more for his country. His remains were brought back to this Post, and interred at the Cemetery in a beautiful grove of oaks.

Never was a braver, better soldier—never was a more loyal, devoted lover of his country—never a man, who had more or stronger friends than Capt. E. C. D. Lines!—*Fort Smith Union.*

The Fort Scott Union Monitor, Extra, brings us a report of a skirmish between part of the troops under Gen. Blunt, and the rebels, in which Capt. Ed. Lines was killed.

He was a son of Hon. Charles B. Lines, Receiver of the Land Office at this place. Capt. Lines entered the army early in the war. He has seen much service—was brave almost to rashness. As an officer he was popular—as a citizen loved and respected by all who knew him—as a son, everything that parents could desire. He, with thousands of others, has laid down his life to perpetuate free institutions.

How many fathers and mothers have been made childless by this war, and are doomed to linger here alone, without the props they had expected would support them in their old age!—*Topeka State Record.*

Tribute to Captain Lines.

A meeting of some of the officers of the 2d Kansas Cavalry was held at Springfield, Mo., September 11th, 1863, to pay tribute to the memory of Capt. E. C. D. Lines, who was killed at the head of his squadron while leading a charge against the enemy near Fort Smith, Arkansas, September 1st, 1863. There were present,

Lieut. Col. Owen A. Bassett, Maj. Julius G. Fisk, Capt. Hugh Cameron, Lieut. John Johnston, Lieut. Elias S. Storer, Lieut. J. Carey French, Lieut. Barnett B Mitchell, Lieut. John B. Dexter, Lieut. Samuel K. Cross. There were also present, by invitation, the following officers of the 2d Indiana Battery: Capt. John W. Rabb, Lieut. Hugh Espey, Lieut. James S. Whicher, they having been with that Battery during the last year, serving with the 2d Kansas Cavalry.

Lieut. J. Carey French was elected to act as Secretary, and a committee was selected to report resolutions. The following were adopted:

WHEREAS, It has pleased Almighty God, in his wisdom, to remove from our midst, our much esteemed and beloved brother officer, Capt. EDWARD C. D. LINES, "C." Co. 2d Kansas Volunteer Cavalry, who died as he lived, brave, true, kind and generous; an accomplished gentleman and honorable soldier, whose bearing, during his long service, has secured the love and esteem of all his brother officers; Therefore,

Resolved, That while we mourn the loss of our departed friend, we feel conscious that his death was that of a true patriot and good soldier, falling as he did, with "his back to the field and feet to the foe."

That dying, as he has lived, faithful in the discharge of his duties, we can proudly point to his example as the pattern of private and official worth and excellence.

That we tender to the afflicted wife and parents of the deceased, our heartfelt sympathies in this, their severe affliction, fully realizing that deeply as we may feel our loss, they mourn a husband and son.

The Secretary was directed to furnish these proceedings to the relatives of the deceased, and for publication in the "Topeka Tribune" and "New Haven Palladium."

J. CAREY FRENCH, *Secretary.*

Testimonials found among the papers of Captain Lines.

HEAD-QUARTERS, 2D REGIMENT, KANSAS VOLUNTEERS.

LEAVENWORTH, KANSAS,
November 11th, 1861.

The bearer of this, Lieut. E. C. D. Lines, has been an officer in our Regiment ever since its organization, and participated in the battles of Forsyth, Dug Springs, and Springfield, in all of which he displayed the most admirable coolness and courage. At Springfield, he was acting Adjutant of the Regiment, and exhibited the most absolute and utter disregard of danger in the discharge of the manifold duties of his position, riding about in the storm of round shot, rifle balls and shell, with the same coolness and self-possession which characterized his conduct on parade or drill.

He is now detached on Recruiting service, and it gives us both pride and pleasure to bear testimony to his worth as a man, and his gallantry as a soldier.

ROBT. B. MITCHELL, Colonel.
CHAS. W. BLAIR, Lieut. Colonel.
W. F. CLOYD, Major.

HEAD-QUARTERS, 30TH BRIGADE, ARMY OF THE OHIO.

IN CAMP NEAR CRAB ORCHARD, KY.,
October 18th, 1862.

MY DEAR SIR.

You are about to leave this command for duty in another field of military operations. My best wishes go with you. As one of the staff of Brig. Gen. Mitchell, you have won from this entire Division the golden opinion which your anxious care to do your whole duty deserved, and you will ever be remembered by all as a brave, capable and faithful officer. I trust you will soon be awarded a rank in which you will have greater opportunity for the exercise of the military ability which you possess. I know that you will acquit yourself well in any position to which you may be assigned, and that the reputation which you have already won in camp and on our severe marches, as well as on the battle field, will never be sullied by any act unbecoming the gallant and accomplished officer. With the most heartfelt wishes for your future success, I have the honor to be,

Very respectfully, your obt. servt.,   P. S. P.

Col. Comdg. 30th Brig., Army of the Ohio.

To Lieut. E. C. D. LINES,
Staff of Gen. Mitchell, 9th Division, Army of the Ohio.

www.ingramcontent.com/pod-product-compliance
Lightning Source LLC
Chambersburg PA
CBHW021456090426
42739CB00009B/1750